P9-EDO-643

Michael Gow was born in Sydney in 1955. He started workshops with the Australian Theatre for Young People in 1970 and joined the Sydney University Dramatic Society in 1975. He lived in London during 1977-78.

Michael's first play, *The Kid*, was workshopped at the Australian National Playwrights' Conference in 1982 and subsequently performed in Sydney, Melbourne, Perth, Canberra, Brisbane and regional cities. He has written for radio and television and in 1985 *The Astronaut's Wife* was produced by the Thalia Theatre Company, of which Michael was a founding member. In 1986 the Sydney Theatre Company premiered *On Top of the World*. In the same year *Away* was premiered by the Griffin Theatre Company and has since been performed widely throughout Australia and also overseas. *Away* won the 1986 NSW Premier's Award for Best Play, the Sydney Theatre Critics' Circle Award and was the outright winner of the 1987 AWGIE Award.

Europe was first performed in 1987 by the Griffin Theatre Company in Sydney. In 1988 The State Theatre Company of South Australia premiered *1841* at the Adelaide Festival and subsequently brought the play to Sydney.

By the same author

The Kid
On Top of the World
Europe
1841

Frontispiece: *Jane Menelaus (Coral) and Jeremy Scrivenbras (Tom) in the State Theatre Company of South Australia production, 1987. Photo by David Wilson.*

AWAY

Michael Gow

CURRENCY   SYDNEY

CURRENCY PLAYS
General Editor: Katharine Brisbane

First published in 1986 by
Currency Press Pty Ltd,
P.O. Box 452 Paddington,
N.S.W. 2021, Australia, in the
Current Theatre Series.
This edition 1988.

Copyright © Michael Gow 1986

This book is copyright. Apart from any fair
dealing for the purpose of private study,
research or review, as permitted under the
Copyright Act, no part may be reproduced by
any process without written permission. Inquiries
concerning publication, translation or recording
rights should be addressed to the publishers.

Any performance or public reading of *Away*
is forbidden unless a licence has been
received from the author or the author's
agent. The purchase of this book in no way
gives the purchaser the right to perform the
play in public, whether by means of a stage
production or a reading. All applications
for public performance should be addressed to
Anthony A. Williams Management Pty Ltd,
First Floor, 50 Oxford Street,
Paddington, N.S.W. 2021

National Library of Australia
Cataloguing-in-Publication data
Gow, Michael.
  Away

  ISBN 0 86819 211 2.

  1. Title.

A822'.3

Typeset by Love Computer Typesetting, Sydney
Printed by Bridge Printery, Sydney

Currency's creative writing program is assisted by the
Australia Council, the Federal Government's arts funding and
advisory body.

'What country, friends, is this?
            Twelfth Night, Act I, sc ii.

'I have done nothing but in care of thee,
    Of thee, my dear one.'
                The Tempest, Act I, sc.ii.

Andrea Moor (Gwen), David Lynch (Jim), Geoff Morrell (Harry) and Julie Godfrey (Vic) in the Griffin Theatre Company production, Sydney 1986. Photo by Francisco Vidinha.

Contents

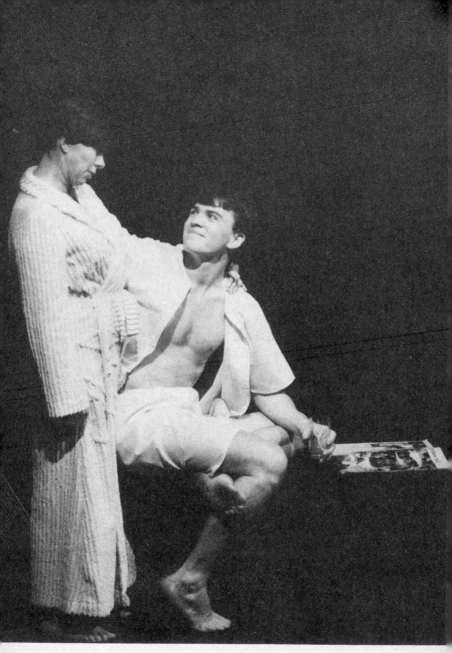

Jenny McNae (Vic) and Richard Dillane (Tom) in the Hole in the Wall Theatre Company production, Perth 1986. Photo by Peter Flanagan.

Introduction

May-Brit Akerholt

Away is set in the summer of 1967-68. Australia was a young nation in the sense that 40% of the population was under 21. By 1968 more than 8000 Australians were fighting in Vietnam and young people were becoming more politically aware. The play ends at the beginning of that year; a 'holiday' is over and around the world 1968 becomes a watershed. Students stage revolts in Paris, Germany and around the United States and focus attention on the bitter debates and splits in Western Society. Censorship in theatre and literature undergoes radical changes. In Australia, plays with four letter words were still banned in most states and actors risked going to gaol for using obscene language. In 1966 the longest running show in Sydney was the revue *A Cup of Tea, a Bex and a Good Lie Down* at the Phillip Street Theatre. By the aquarian generation in 1969 *Hair* had taken over. The holiday was indeed over for Australia.

The portrayal of Australia in *Away* is as ironic as the title of Donald Horne's *The Lucky Country*. Gow's characters are imprisoned in a world in which their worth as human beings is measured in the cost of their holidays. To preserve a way of life means sending their sons to fight America's war in Vietnam; to celebrate Christmas means hot dinners and plastic trees; the aim is to be the same as everyone else, as long as that means to be better than one's neighbour. Gwen's attitude to life echoes Girlie Pogson in Patrick White's *The Season at Sarsaparilla*: 'I like a hat to look different so long as it's what the others are wearing.' But, like all works which have an enduring quality, Gow's play dramatises a universal world through one which is limited by time and space. And like many recent Australian plays, such as Patrick White's *Shepherd on the Rocks*, David Malouf's *Blood Relations* and Louis Nowra's *The Golden Age*, *Away* is about reconciliation and the power of healing through love and compassion.

Away is historical in the sense that it places its characters and themes within a particular society and draws on the mood and spirit of a particular era to portray a larger world. It is a play about families — the young generation and their parents — and a play about the world we live in. The three families go away on their annual holidays, but their journey becomes a theatrical metaphor for a spiritual quest. As in classical Greek and Shakespearean drama, the purpose of the quest is to gain self-knowledge. Thus *Away* is essentially about coming home, or undertaking a journey from ignorance to knowledge; from blindness to insight. At the end, the characters have a new understanding of the world around them because they have accepted the motives, ambitions, hopes and fears which determine their actions. This journey is embedded in the character of Coral, who links the school play with a Shakespearean world of distortion, the tragedy of lost hopes and the possibility of restoring order through love. She sees the darkness within Tom, the bruises of his illness and the image of death behind his vitality.

Away belongs to a growing tradition which integrates other sources into the fabric of new works. But in its very use of classical material, the play is of a classical nature. From the times of the ancient Greeks through to the Renaissance, legends and foreign literary works were introduced into local art forms and became part of an indigenous body of works. The fact that *Away*, as he has himself pointed out, is set at the time of Gow's own early adolescence means that he is dealing with a period he can now see in perspective. The Shakespearean connotations provide a retrospective view in the same way that looking at events from a distance and in the light of a wider knowledge and experience can heighten the understanding and meaning of those events. The resonances brought to the action by classic texts add a dimension to the characters' reality. The magic rites of *A Midsummer Night's Dream* and the fairies' tempest enhance the events of ordinary lives and take them beyond the realm of surface experience. We see the characters in terms of magic and poetry, as if their own lives gain new meaning through dreams and visions played out on stage. Another Australia emerges, a country which is no longer an isolated island but part of an extended world. It has the beauty and freshness of a new world and the wisdom and mythology of a very old one.

On the one hand, the scene from *A Midsummer Night's Dream* which opens the play tells us that life is filled with mystery and poetry, but on the other, the scene's execution by a group of high school students adds a measure of humour and irony to the statement. In the middle of fairy lights and tripping fantastical school-elves appears Puck, as if by magic, but he is soon revealed to be Tom, their own Chips Rafferty.

Just as Puck 'directs' the dance of the fairies in the school performance, so it is that Tom's character channels the play's action. Within the mythology of *Away* it is Tom who conjures up the fairies' tempest which destroys the caravan park, as if in terrible revenge on injustice and insularity; and it is the tempest which brings the families together on a secluded, unspoilt beach. It is Tom who creates a magic play for amateur night, a play about loss and hope which restores Coral to life. At the end of the play, Tom reads the role of King Lear, bringing death into life, with the paradox that in death there is reconciliation and hope. This play about the experiences of a dying schoolboy is a celebration of life and the power to heal through gaining insight. It is a celebration of sun, sand, water and fire, the vital energies of Australia, energies which have the power both to destroy and to restore.

The theme in *King Lear* of blindness and healing through a journey of division, pain and death, is also the theme of *The Stranger on the Shore*, the playlet performed by Tom and Coral on amateur night. It functions as a tragic interlude, a play-within-the-play which deals with love, sacrifice and death. In showing Coral how to walk again, it tells all the characters how to find their way home after their time away from themselves and each other. It also tells Tom's parents not to grieve; they must suffer the loss of their son, but they have shown him 'how to walk' while he lived. The scene ends in an image of cleansing and purification: the red glow of a bonfire on the beach.

Tom's playlet gives perspective to Harry's speech in Act IV i in which the father tries to see his son's inevitable death in the light of a larger scheme. He points to the Chinese belief that to grieve too much when someone dies means that their life was unfinished and that they had not achieved enough to be worthy of death. Harry's tribute to his son is to accept death: 'in a funny way we're happy. Even while we're very, very sad.'

These lines also sum up the tone of the play as well as the feeling the audience retains at the end; a feeling of simultaneous elation and sorrow. The characters' self-deception is portrayed through comedy, but the humour is counterpointed both by a dark tone of longing and bitterness, of unattainable dreams and lost ambitions, and by a lyrical tone of magic and beauty, which in this play expresses the poetry of life. Throughout the play, comic and serious scenes are juxtaposed, and each scene contains a mixture of light and dark tones. Gow infuses the serious themes with a comic vision; he finds both the ridiculous and the tragic in ordinary people and everyday events. The character of Gwen is genuinely funny as the stereotypical nagging wife and mother, the pretentious snob whose aspirations are symbolised by a caravan with all the comforts of her suburban home. But her actions and language are like an armour hiding pain and fear as tangible and as destructive as Tom's illness.

The comedy in the amateur night scene lies partly in the send-up of typical holiday camp entertainment, partly in the way the characters respond to it. The playlet performed by Tom and Coral is also funny, and stage directions such as 'CORAL *makes ship noises on a bottle*' and '*She swoons*' specify the comic aspects of the performance. But the comedy is gradually undermined by the tragic implications until the scene has moved from tired jokes and a rendition of *Pearly Shells* accompanied on the ukulele, to Coral's line 'I'm walking, I'm walking' to the tune of Mendelssohn's Nocturne.

The structure of the dialogue works in the same way as the tone, emphasising themes and action. Short, quick lines, usually duologues, in which the characters respond to each other's words without really listening to their meaning alternate with lyrical passages which reveal the characters' feelings and inner lives. Repetition of words and phrases emphasises the emptiness of their social language, and of the personal language they create to avoid confronting what might lie beneath the surface meaning of the words they speak.

When confrontation does take place, the characters' worlds fall apart. But it is a necessary destruction, bringing the characters together on a 'magical' beach to be restored and reconciled. Coral's escape from Roy and the glittering Gold Coast hotel leads her to the healing powers of nature and Tom. Gwen, Jim and Meg are ravaged by the forces of nature on Christmas day, by a fierce tempest brought by the fairies of the school play — and Puck/Tom. The storm destroys a whole way of life as it tears at the family's belongings; a way of life dramatised in the chorus of campers and emphasised by Mendelssohn's Wedding March. (Richard Wherrett's Sydney Theatre Company production brought out the central role of Gwen in this scene by having her buffeted by the wind as she clung to her possessions. The fairies also appeared battered and torn, embodiments of the characters' inner lives as they journeyed through the storm.) In the next scene the storm is replaced by the almost dreamlike stillness of a sun-filled beach and Mendelssohn's *Midsummer Night's Dream* music.

The quest undertaken by the characters in *Away* brings them home to the same old world but with a renewed sense of reality. The characters have moved from the artificial lights of the school hall through the distorted landscape of Shakespeare to scenes set in nature. The more the characters reveal themselves, the closer they move to nature. We last see them under the trees in the schoolyard reading *King Lear*: 'it is the power of nature, its participation in the drama' which illuminates 'the struggle between man and nature, as well as between man and man, and between man and himself.' As Tom reads from the opening speech, he is setting his role in the play in perspective: 'While we/Unburden'd crawl towards death.'

                                                        Sydney, 1988

The Play on the Stage

Richard Wherrett

When I first saw the Griffin Theatre production of *Away* at the Stables in January 1986 I was immediately struck by three things: this was a wonderful night in the theatre; the play was deserving of being seen by more people than those who could fit into the 140-seat space in six weeks and the play had the potential to be served by production resources far more expansive than the Stables could provide. Most audiences shared my delight: the season at the Stables was packed out, and these 6,000 people were clearly only a sample of a vast audience potential. The Sydney Theatre Company season at the Drama Theatre in 1987 was seen by a further 22,320 people, and since then *Away* has been seen in theatres right across the country.

It is a rare work that can fit comfortably into any venue. One of the key factors in the success of a production is the suitability of the venue in which it is produced: an intimate space for a chamber work, an expansive one for an epic work. The essential qualities of *Away* — its lyricism, the simplicity of its staging demands, and the economy of its line and form — mean that it can very easily be realised on a small scale with minimum production attributes. On the other hand while the play begins apparently naturalistically, the 'away' to which the three families go for their summer break is a world where anything can happen — a dreamscape (as in *A Midsummer Night's Dream*), a sanctuary (as in *As You Like It*), and a danger zone (as in *The Tempest*) — and as such provides vast scope for theatrical, magical and fantastic effects. This flexibility is a producer's delight and the range of production scope a director's dream.

There is a similar range possible in the cast size of the play. While the doubling as suggested by the original production makes conceptual sense (as well as economic sense), I would love to see a production in which Leonie, Miss Latrobe, and the MC were played by additional cast members. This would provide two distinct advantages: it would accentuate the doubling of Tom/Rick which is valuable insofar as Coral sees both Tom and Rick as her lost son; and it would provide a handful more fairies to permeate the play, to wreak joy and despair on the holidaymakers in the same apparently arbitrary way that nature does in life. In particular the storm scene of III iv asks for a deluge of fairies and panoply of effects. And while, in keeping with the naive production style, which the opening scene (from *A Midsummer Night's Dream*) seems to demand, these effects can be produced by thunder sheets, wind and rain machines, wind fans, water pistols and so on (ideally all clearly visible), there is every reason why they might also be reinforced by the modern technology of sound tapes, lighting effects, 'flying' fairies and so on. The maximum chaos here finds its natural and deeply touching counterpoise in the tranquility of the following scene which ends the first half of the play. A bigger cast would add reinforcements to the hotel guests, campers, and school students who people other scenes. And I was particularly taken by the idea of hinting at the possibility that the malevolent campers of III iii might also be fairies. A good-sized band of mischievous fairies has indeed a delicious if expensive appeal.

It is a rare work, too, that has within it the flexibility to be interpreted in a variety of ways. I believe a great work is one that will continue to be produced beyond its time. A criterion of this continued life is the universality of the subject matter, the capacity of the themes to speak to any place at any time, and in turn to be reinterpreted in terms of any place and any time. The central subjects of *Away*—regeneration, recreation, restoration, resolution, and resignation—are universal ones which find some of their most profound expression in Shakespeare, from whom Gow draws his inspiration.

The recreation we seek from a holiday is the restoration of our physical and spiritual energies, our life forces. Tom, Harry and Vic are arguably the only characters who 'don't look forward' (Harry, IV i). They live resolutely in the present, the only time they have as a family under the threat to Tom's health. The remaining characters, with the exception of Meg, are either 'holding back', 'keeping in' or 'hanging on to' the past, which is a kind of death; just as the future, with the threat of loss and abandonment appears also to be a kind of death. The future is the unknown and to embrace it requires a letting go of whatever it is that binds us to the past. To do this is to be free. To hang on is to be asleep ('like in a dream': Rick, III iii). To be awake is the way to face reality: it then becomes an easy thing to let go. Thus *a* way can become *the* way. In its many ways, *Away* is an affirmation of these basic human needs.

The structure of the play reinforces these themes and in this way form coheres with content, which is I believe a measure of art. The play begins indoors, within the confines of small domestic interiors. The first scenes away open out a little — a Surfers Paradise Hotel ballroom, a crowded 'caravan city', the roof top of the hotel. The end of Act III finds us at a beach, *the* beach of Tom, Harry and Vic, and releases us into a vast open space — endless sand, vaulted sky, a place to relish freedom. We never again retreat indoors. The final scene of the play, again set outdoors, brings us full circle as Tom and his classmates undertake the first reading of their new text, *King Lear*. The last lines exploit dramatic irony in masterful poignancy as Tom and we the audience reel from his words, while his friends read on unwittingly.

Tom is central to these themes. Imbued with a sense of his own mortality, he is inspired despite his pain to lead others out of theirs. Puck-like, he is the play's protagonist, mentor, engineer, lifeline, and radiance. He is the catalyst to the situation and its salvation. The play gains accordingly by being delightfully funny, distinctly resonant, and deeply moving.

Sydney, April 1988

Above: Carole Skinner (Gwen) and Catherine McClements (Meg) in the State Theatre Company of South Australia production 1987. Photo by David Wilson. Below: Andy King (Jim) and Fiona Gauntlett (Meg) in the Hole in the Wall Theatre Company production, Perth 1986. Photo by Peter Flanagan.

Above: Sally Cooper (Meg) and Paul Goddard (Tom) in the Playbox Theatre Company production, Melbourne 1986. Photo by Jeff Busby. Below: David Lynch (Jim) and Geoff Morrell (Harry) in the Griffin Theatre Company production, Sydney 1986. Photo by Francisco Vidinha.

Above: Jane Harders (Coral) and Steven Vidler (Tom) in the Sydney Theatre Company production 1987. Photo by Sandy Edwards. Below: Jillian Murray (Vic), Ross Williams (Harry) and Julia Blake (Coral) in the Playbox Theatre Company production 1986. Photo by Jeff Busby.

Above: Don Barker (Roy) and Jane Menelaus (Coral) in the State Theatre Company of South Australia production 1987. Photo by David Wilson. Below: Julia Blake (Coral) and Alan Cassell (Roy) in the Playbox Theatre Company production 1986. Photo by Jeff Busby.

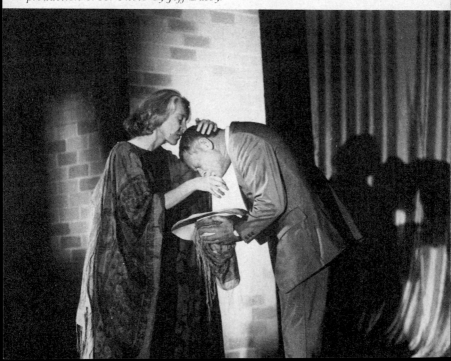

Away was first performed by the Griffin Theatre Company on 7 January 1986 at the Stables Theatre, Sydney, with the following cast:

TOM	Christian Hodge
ROY	Benjamin Franklin
MEG	Angela Toohey
GWEN	Andrea Moor
JIM	David Lynch
CORAL	Vanessa Downing
HARRY	Geoff Morrell
VIC	Julie Godfrey
LEONIE	Angela Toohey
RICK	Christian Hodge

Campers, hotel guests, fairies etc. were played by the company.

Directed by Peter Kingston
Designed by Robert Kemp
Lighting design by Liz Allen

CHARACTERS

TOM/RICK
ROY/HOTEL GUEST/ FIRST CAMPER/MC
MEG/LEONIE
GWEN/HOTEL GUEST
JIM/HOTEL GUEST
CORAL/SECOND CAMPER HARRY/HOTEL GUEST/THIRD
  CAMPER
VIC/HOTEL GUEST/FOURTH CAMPER/MISS LATROBE

Summer 1967-68

ACT ONE

SCENE ONE

A school performance of A Midsummer Night's Dream *is coming to a close. The Mendelssohn soundtrack blares from a tinny loudspeaker. Kids dressed as fairies scurry about in garish light. The music ends and the fairies strike a tableau. One of them,* TOM, *steps forward and addresses the audience.*

TOM: If we shadows have offended,
  Think but this, and all is mended,
  That you have but slumbered here
  While these visions did appear.
  And this weak and idle theme,
  No more yielding but a dream,
  Gentles, do not reprehend.
  If you pardon, we will mend.
  And, as I am an honest Puck,
  If we have unearnèd luck
  Now to scrape the serpent's tongue,
  We will make amends ere long;
  Else the Puck a liar call.
  So, good night unto you all.
  Give me your hands, if we be friends,
  And Robin shall restore amends.

Music again, the FAIRIES *scurry about and the curtain closes. It opens again and they are caught unready. They form a line and bow a few times, the curtain closes again and they wander off.* ROY *comes to the curtains. They open a little and he addresses the audience.*

ROY: Well, I'm sure you all enjoyed the little show tonight. What a lot of little Chips Rafferties we've got here in our own school. Now there are a few people I'd like to say a few words of thanks to before we go tonight. Allan and Betty Shirlaw for providing the timber and so on at cost to build the settings, Joy Samuels and the Art Department for painting it all and making it look so terrific. Seymours for providing the cordials at half time. Mrs Walker for the luscious cakes, well done Lois. Mrs Hutton, Mrs Cooper, Mrs Lummis and Mrs Papa . . . Papalapa . . . Papalax . . . oh well, I'm sure she knows who I mean, ha ha ha, for making the outfits . . . Finally Miss Latrobe, the person responsible for getting the whole show together you've seen here tonight, as well as getting our debating team into the quarter finals. Thank you, Miss Latrobe. Well, that about wraps it up so thank you all for coming and have a safe and happy Christmas and best wishes for nineteen-sixty-eight. Thank you.

[*He moves away, then remembers something.*]

Oh, and one more thing. A message from Charlie. Please watch the flowering beds as you leave the school, we lost quite a few at prize-giving night. Thank you.

SCENE TWO

Backstage. TOM *and* MEG.

TOM: You going away tomorrow?
MEG: We're leaving really early.
TOM: Well . . . have a good time.
MEG: Where are you going?
TOM: Up the coast. Some beach.
MEG: Have a good time.
TOM: Bound to.
MEG: See you.
TOM: Yeah . . . see you in pictures.
MEG: You too.
TOM: No thanks.
MEG: You were really good in the play.
TOM: Bull.
MEG: You were!
TOM: Cut it out. I'll get a fat head.
MEG: My olds are waiting.
TOM: Anyway, I got this for you. As a memento of the play.
MEG: Thanks.

TOM: It was a real laugh being in the play with you.

MEG: No-o . . .

TOM: It was! So I got you something as a token of my appreciation.

MEG: What is it?

TOM: If you open it up you might find out. It's a piece of junk, actually. Actually I nicked it. But it's the thought that counts.

MEG: You nicked it?

TOM: Actually, I got a night job and slogged me guts out for ten years to pay for it.

MEG: A brooch.

TOM: A mere bauble.

MEG: It's really nice. That's really nice of you.

TOM: Oh, stop before you start sobbing.

MEG: I really like it.

TOM: It's from the bottom of my heart, actually.

MEG: I wish I'd got you something.

TOM: I have some beautiful memories.

MEG: Oh yuck.

TOM: Sick, eh?

MEG: It was good fun, though. Pity it was only for one night. Fancy doing it night after night like in America. Plays go on for years there. London too. Wouldn't you get sick of it?

TOM: Depends who else was in it. Be great if you hated everyone's guts.

MEG: But then it'd only be the same as a proper job.

TOM: What are you going to be when you grow up?

MEG: An engine driver. You?

TOM: I'll wait and see.

MEG: I'd better be going. Thanks for the brooch.

TOM: It matches your eyes.

MEG: Yellow?

TOM: Joke

MEG: Ha ha.

TOM: Sorry.

MEG: Well . . .

TOM: The olds.

MEG: Have a good Christmas.

TOM: Don't go yet.

MEG: Why?

TOM: This is fun.

MEG: What is?

TOM: Trying to think of things to say.

MEG: We haven't done the weather yet.

TOM: Do you really like the brooch?

MEG: Yep.

TOM: Good.

MEG: I really like it.

TOM: It was either jewellery or perfume. But it's hard to buy perfume for someone you don't know very well. You need to know their personal chemical make up. I could have got something on spec and it mightn't have worked on you and you'd have to put it on and stunk like a dead dog. You wouldn't have been able to wash it off, either. You have to wait till something like that fades. You wouldn't be so nice about me in the play then, eh? My name'd be mud. That's why I went for jewellery. Safer. Better bet. Actually I asked around a few places. Got a bit of advice. Shop girls and that.

MEG: And they said jewellery?

TOM: Most of them. They said I should opt for the jewellery. A few suggested some perfume. Very subtle stuff. Couldn't actually smell it. One of them tried some on and I was halfway down her neck before any smell registered. Pointless.

MEG: Well . . . I still wish I'd got you something.

TOM: Bottle of gin would've been nice.

MEG: Oh.

TOM: Or a Harley Davidson.

MEG: Is he a poet?

TOM: It's a bike.

MEG: I knew that.

TOM: Poet! Why would I want a poet?

MEG: Maybe you read poetry.

TOM: Me? Come on! Me?

MEG: You might. You're pretty . . .

TOM: Deep?

MEG: You're pretty quiet.

TOM: Soulful?

MEG: Still waters run deep. My father's always saying that.

TOM: Still waters stink.

[GWEN *and* JIM *come in.*]

GWEN: You were supposed to hurry, not stand round yapping. There are a million things to do. I'll have to do it all, I expect.

TOM: 'Ill met by moonlight'.

GWEN: I beg your pardon? Are you a friend of Margaret's? I didn't know you were a friend of this boy's, Margaret.

MEG: Not really.

TOM: No, not really.

MEG: Until the play.

TOM: Yeah. Until the play, that is.

MEG: Did you like the play, Dad?

JIM: It was . . . lovely, yes.

GWEN: What did you have to do Shakespeare for? Why couldn't you have done a musical? A bit of singing. All that talking! And we couldn't see a thing. The people in front kept hopping up and down, up and down to see. We couldn't see a blessed thing. We just managed to see a bit of the queen's crown. And there were these kids near us, why you'd bring kiddies to stuff like this I do not know, but — muck-up? I could've throttled them. Little beggars. But whose idea was it to do Shakespeare? Very silly choice if you ask me.

JIM: You looked lovely though, Mags. And you'll be our next Chips Rafferty, eh, son?

TOM: Don't hold your breath.

GWEN: We can't spend all night here. Not if you two want any sort of holiday. Say your goodnights, Margaret. Have you got the keys?

JIM: Keys? I thought I gave them to you.

GWEN: No, I gave them to you. To get the camera out of the car. Why, I do not know. We couldn't see a thing. We were so far back you couldn't get a photo of anything. You always have to bring it. But you kept the keys.

JIM: Did I?

GWEN: Yes.

JIM: I don't think so. They're not on me.

GWEN: They must be. Trouser pockets.

JIM: No, no I'm sure you still have them. They're not there.

GWEN: I do not believe this. I know I gave them to you. I remember. I gave you the camera and then the keys. I said, 'Here's your stupid camera, it'll be a waste bringing it' and I handed you the keys. Oh honestly.

JIM: Don't worry. Don't start to worry.

GWEN: I know I haven't got them.

JIM: I ... no I haven't. I don't remember. But we'll find them. Just don't get upset.

GWEN: Well, where are they?!

JIM: Don't get upset.

GWEN: I have not got them.

[*She tips the contents of her handbag on the floor.*]

There! Are they there? Can you see a set of keys? I can't. Can anyone see a set of keys?

JIM: Well, they must be around. We'll find them. Don't get upset.

GWEN: Look! There are no keys there.

[*She picks things up and shoves them in the bag again.*]

No. No. No. No. No. No. No. I haven't come across any keys yet.

[ROY *and* CORAL *come in.*]

JIM: Oh dear. Here they are. Back pocket. Goodness me. What a duffer.

GWEN: I did not have the keys. Did I? Now my eyes are stinging. I can hardly see. It hurts. I need a Bex.

ROY: Any good shots?

JIM: A couple, I think.

GWEN: Of course not. We were so far back. Hullo. We thought we'd lost the keys.

[*Awkward pause.*]

ROY: So what do you think of our little Chips Rafferties, eh? Proud mums and dads?

GWEN: I wish they'd done a musical. My head.

ROY: It ... er ... it was hot in that hall. We might see the P. and C. about some air conditioning next year. Very

stuffy. It's a pity they weren't selling something a bit
stronger than cordial. Made a killing.
  [*Pause.*]
Very stuffy. When you said that bit about you have
slumbered here you were certainly hitting the nail on the
head. Not that I was bored. No. It was a good night out.
  [*Pause.*]
Off away, are you?

JIM: In the morning.

GWEN: If we ever get a start. [*To* CORAL] Did you enjoy the
play?
  [CORAL *stares at her for a moment then looks away.*]
We were right at the back. Wasn't the music lovely?
  [*Pause.*]
Have you been well?
  [CORAL *doesn't respond.* HARRY *and* VIC *come in.*]

HARRY: Here he is, Vic! He's here. There you are.

VIC: Where is he? There you are. Ahhhhhh, well done.
There's my boy. Weren't you marvellous? You were
marvellous.

HARRY: Congratulations, son. A real Laurence Olivier you
are.

VIC: Oh, it was marvellous. Wasn't it a lovely show?

GWEN: Oh, yes.

JIM: Very nice.

VIC: You looked so wicked, Tom.

HARRY: I said to your mother, our Tom's got a bit of
hobgoblin in him. Where did he get that then, eh?
  [HARRY *and* VIC *laugh.*]

VIC: But we did enjoy it. Very much. You should be proud,
Mr Baker. This has done the school a lot of good. Brought
a lot of happiness.

ROY: Oh, yes, yes. It has been a successful evening.

HARRY: You're not tired, son?

TOM: Full of beans.

HARRY: You sure?

VIC: Leave him. This is his hour of triumph. [*To* MEG] You
were lovely too.

MEG: Thanks.

VIC: Wasn't she lovely? You must be proud.

JIM: Yes, we are.

GWEN: Oh, yes.

VIC: Oh, it did us good.

HARRY: What a way to end the year. Marvellous.

ROY: You going away?

HARRY: Oh . . . we're going to drive for a bit. See what we find.

ROY: You seen much of this country yet? How long have you been out here?

VIC: Eight years. Not a lot of it, no, not yet.

HARRY: We will, though.

GWEN: You caravanning?

HARRY: Ohhh . . . no. Not exactly. We've got a tent.

JIM: Oh, a tent. Terrific. I miss the old tent sometimes.

GWEN: We've got a new caravan. Everything in it you could want.

JIM: If you need a couple of stretchers . . .

HARRY: It's a small tent. We just put it up against the car.

GWEN: A lean-to?

HARRY: That's it.

GWEN: Ohhhhh.

ROY: Well, we've got a plane to catch. The Gold Coast.

VIC: Oh, lovely.

GWEN: The Gold Coast . . . well. You'll have a lovely time.

ROY: We'll see you all next year. Last year for you two, eh? A good Christmas, then.

ALL: Goodnight. Safe journey. Cheerio. *etc*.

[ROY *and* CORAL *go*.]

GWEN: She looks awful, poor woman. Her son, you know.

VIC: Yes. We heard.

GWEN: Poor woman.

HARRY:Time we were in bed, I think.

GWEN: Have a lovely time in your . . . tent.

VIC: We'll be fine. Won't we?

TOM: I think I'll walk home.

HARRY: You got a jumper?

VIC: He's all right. Don't be too long. Goodnight.

JIM:
GWEN: } Yes, goodnight. Have a good trip.

TOM: See you.

MEG: Goodnight, Tom. Thanks for the brooch.

[HARRY *and* VIC *and* TOM *go.*]

GWEN: What brooch?

MEG: He gave me a brooch.

GWEN: What for?

MEG: I don't know. He liked being in the play.

GWEN: He's a bit . . . no hopery.

MEG: He's all right.

GWEN: They both work, don't they? In a factory, isn't it? I'm sure that's what I heard. A lean-to. They shouldn't be going on a holiday if they can't afford one.

[TOM *runs back in. He has heard this.*]

TOM: I hope you have a rotten holiday. I hope it rains. I hope the dunnies overflow and you all get the runs. I hope you get sunstroke and end up in hospital. I hope all the fish you catch are poisoned. I hope you have a fucken miserable time.

[*He goes.*]

GWEN: Where do they live?

MEG: It doesn't matter

GWEN: I want to know. They have no special privileges. No one asked them to come out to this country. They have no right to behave any differently.

MEG: He's just excited tonight. You were awful.

GWEN: Was I? Was I? Awful. Some people may be happy living like pigs but I'm not. I will not have you hanging around with that kind of life.

MEG: What kind of life?

GWEN: Motor bikes. Tattoos. Drink. A sad, dirty life. Unless you'd rather live like that? If that's the case you'd better speak up now. Let us know now so your father can stop slaving in that office and we can both stop killing ourselves to give you everything. My head will split.

[*She stalks out.* MEG *and* JIM *follow her.*]

SCENE THREE

Outside. CORAL, *alone.*

CORAL: When that woman woke up and saw that donkey at
her feet I thought my heart would break. I had to wipe
away tears. To wake up and find something you want so
badly. Even an animal. And then she woke up again and
saw her husband and loved him. That boy! In that blue
light the shadows on his face and neck were like bruises.
He looked so sick yet so wonderful, so white, so cold and
burning. 'What angel wakes me from my flowery bed?'
I kept saying it over and over in the dark. All these children,
having fun, playing and me sitting there in the dark wiping
away tears. I could hardly watch them. Their legs and arms
painted gold. And that boy's hair, so black. And his smile.
'What angel wakes me from my flowery bed?' Is it better
for them to die like that? Looking like gods? Burning, gold,
white. What's that word they always say in those plays?
Alas?

[*She sighs.*]

Alas.

[ROY *comes in.*]

ROY: I thought I told you to wait in the car.

CORAL: I was hot. Just walking.

ROY: Let's get home.

CORAL: I'm hot.

ROY: We'll have a drink when we get home.

CORAL: I was just walking.

[*They go.*]

ACT TWO

SCENE ONE

At home. HARRY *and* TOM.

TOM: You didn't have to wait up for me.
HARRY: There's still a lot to do, you know.
TOM: I was all right.
HARRY: Last minute things.
TOM: I got home in one piece, didn't I?
HARRY: I think your mother'll need a trailer for her stuff.
TOM: I won't need much.
HARRY: You feeling all right?
TOM: I'm not tired. I feel wide awake.
HARRY: You looking forward to this trip?
TOM: Of course I am.
HARRY: We are.
TOM: We've been talking about it for months.
HARRY: It'll be a good break.
TOM: That's right. I'm thirsty.
HARRY: We need a good break. From home, work.
TOM: You want a drink?
HARRY: A cup of tea?
TOM: I feel like something cold.
HARRY: It's been a rough year.
TOM: I remember, you know.
HARRY: On your mother.
TOM: Yes, I do know that. I remember it all.
HARRY: So you can forgive us looking forward to this little
    trip?
TOM: Have I complained? Why do you think I don't want
    to go?
HARRY: Planning the holidays was as important to your
    mother as actually going away.
TOM: I want to go.
HARRY: Something to look forward to.
TOM: Same for me.

HARRY: A few weeks just with ourselves. Just with you. It'll be good.

TOM: It'll be terrific. I've looked forward to it. Ever since you suggested it I've wanted to go. That day in the hospital and you brought in the tent and put it up in the ward. I couldn't wait for summer to come.

HARRY: When you have your own kids you'll know what I'm talking about.

TOM: Come on, Dad, you're getting tired.

HARRY: When you've got your own family —

TOM: Do you want a drink or not?

HARRY: Put the jug on.

TOM: No. I want something cold.

HARRY: It's not going to be a flash holiday.

TOM: I don't want to go to St. Tropez.

HARRY: But it will be fun. Most of the time.

TOM: It'll be a laugh a minute.

HARRY: And even if it does get a bit dull, a bit boring, even if you do get a bit fed up, you know a bit . . . pissed off . . .

TOM: Shit, Dad, where did you pick that up?

HARRY: Even if it is slow, if you could try and still have a good time, look like you're having a good time. I'm asking this for your mother. It's for her. Let her see you really enjoying yourself, having a terrific time.

TOM: I won't have to try.

HARRY: I'm not asking you to lie.

TOM: I wouldn't. But I won't need to.

HARRY: But . . . well, you are a bit of a Laurence Olivier. We were very proud tonight. I glanced sideways at your mother at one point and her face was glowing, it was shining. She was very happy.

TOM: You'll be tired tomorrow. You'll fall asleep at the wheel. Then where will we be? Some holiday.

HARRY What about that cup of tea?

TOM: I think I'll go to bed.

HARRY: Don't get too tired, will you?

TOM: That's why I'm going to bed.

HARRY: We love you a lot.

TOM: You shouldn't worry about me. Now hit the sack.

HARRY: Have you got your mother a present?
TOM: I got three. They get bigger and better.
HARRY: I'll see you in the morning.

SCENE TWO

GWEN *and* MEG.

GWEN: Margaret? Do you want these flippers to go?
MEG: Yes.
GWEN: Well, do you think they'll pack themselves? Do you think holidays happen by themselves?
MEG: No.
GWEN: Well, get those pillow slips. And I can't see any beach towels here. I hope no one expects to take any of my good towels down onto the beach. Did you hear me?
MEG: Yes. I'll get some now.
GWEN: Is that box of canned food out at the car? It should go in the boot.
MEG: [*off, calling*] Mum wants to know if the box of groceries has gone out.
JIM: [*off, calling*] Yes. It's here.
MEG: Yes, it's there.
GWEN: Miracle of miracles. My head will split. Look how late it is. We won't get enough sleep. And we won't get away before seven. Every lunatic on earth will be on the roads in the morning. [*Calling*] I said every lunatic on earth will be on the roads tomorrow. And we'll be caught in the middle of it. [*Back to* MEG] I wish some people did a bit more, with a bit more preparation. Instead of leaving it all to the last second. People think holidays happen all by themselves.
MEG: I think you should go to bed now.
GWEN: Ha! We'd still be here on New Year's Day. No, I'll keep going. I may as well.
MEG: But your head's killing you.
GWEN: I'll have a Bex before bed.
MEG: But why not stop, rest, relax? We'll get there.

GWEN: Have you got the Thermos organised yet?

MEG: I'll do it, don't worry.

GWEN: I may as well be talking to a lot of brick walls. And what have you packed in the way of clothes? You're old enough to cope with that. I suppose you are. It's up to you. Just don't come running to me when you've got nothing to wear. I told you two weeks ago, as soon as your exams were finished and over with, to start getting your things together.

MEG: Yes, I've done it. I've got a bag. Why can't you relax?

GWEN: Don't take on that tone of voice. You'll end up a snide miss and no one can stand that. Everyone does what they have to. If we're going to have any sort of reasonable holiday we're going to have to pay for it. We're paying for it now, by spending all night packing up to go.

MEG: But it doesn't seem much fun.

GWEN: Fun. Now there's a good word. Fun. It doesn't seem much fun.

MEG: You aren't enjoying it. Have you ever enjoyed it?

GWEN: Why don't you go and live with your friend for a while, then, if you want to have fun all the time? They look like they always have fun. Nothing to show for it, of course, but if it's fun that you're after then you go right ahead. This case won't close.

MEG: I'll sit on it.

[*They struggle with the case until it is shut.*]

GWEN: My head is spinning.

MEG: Go to bed.

[JIM *comes in.*]

Make her go to bed.

JIM: Is that the lot?

MEG: Just this case.

JIM: We're ready to roll, then.

GWEN: Ha! There'll be something. There always is.

MEG: Go to bed.

GWEN: I'm going to have a powder, then I'll be off. Take that case out tonight.

[*She goes.*]

MEG: When you're married to someone, do you ever wish they were dead?

JIM: Please don't be hard towards your mother.

MEG: If you spend a long time with one person don't you ever wish you could be rid of them?

JIM: You mustn't expect too much from her.

MEG: Do you expect much from her?

JIM: No.

MEG: Do you expect anything from her?

JIM: She is very worried about that boy in the play. He hasn't got a hold over you, has he? Tell me if he has.

MEG: He doesn't have a hold over me.

JIM: He's never been around you, all these years of school, then suddenly you're in this play and all we hear is Tom this, Tom that, Tom said, Tom thinks. We notice.

MEG: You worry too much.

JIM: Your mother thinks I don't worry enough.

MEG: I'm not having a baby.

JIM: I know that.

MEG: That's what you're really asking.

JIM: Not only that. You might be drawn away, pulled away from us. That would be very upsetting.

MEG: I won't stay here forever.

JIM: But you mustn't go at the wrong time, with the wrong person.

MEG: Wrong?

JIM: Don't abandon your mother.

MEG: I won't.

JIM: Everything has been so good up 'til now, everything has gone so well. Don't just walk away.

MEG: I don't understand. Mum has a great story she tells once a year or so. About growing up in a country town. About all her brothers and sisters and her parents. How one day she realised she was expected to stay at home forever and look after them. She knew then she had to get out. So she packed her bags and got a train. She was eighteen, I think, or nineteen. She left. Like that, in a minute. She never went back for eight years. They wouldn't speak to her. She got married and they came down for the wedding and stayed a couple of days. Then you saw them once a year if they were lucky. When I was born, maybe twice a year. She never writes, never rings. They could die and she wouldn't find out for months. Isn't that wanting to abandon someone? Wasn't she pulled away? Did you stay?

JIM: Life was so much harder.

MEG: You got out. You packed up and hit the road for years. You tell a story too. You got out. You were pulled away.

JIM: It was money. It was bread. Work. The world was full of people walking around the countryside looking for something to eat, all thinking about the day they could stop walking. We all did it. Your mother did it. When we met we thought about it together. We lived in rubbish tips. We shared rooms with other people. Everyone did. And we all planned. We planned our time. We waited. We stuck to our plans like the Bible. And we're getting there. That was a time of complete madness when we think back. There was no order, no plan. We got through one day, then we got through the next, then the next. My plans were for me, but your mother ... hers are for all of us. You have no idea how hard she has stuck to them, how she has fought to get where we are. And her plans are the way we have to go. It's as if she can see into the future. We have to support her, follow her, stick to her plans.

MEG: I want to be certain like that.

JIM: And you are so important to your mother's plans.

MEG: But I'm not.

JIM: I wish we'd said no to that play.

MEG: If I'd played volley ball I'd still feel like this. I don't think you should have given in all the time. I think you've been cheated.

JIM: No.

MEG: I don't think anyone should give in for the sake of peace and quiet. I won't.

JIM: I'd like you to promise to be patient. Just a bit longer, a few more years, let things take their course.

MEG: If we don't get up early we'll be in a lot of trouble.

JIM: Good girl.

MEG: I'm not. I'm only tired.

SCENE THREE

ROY *and* CORAL.

ROY: Two things!

CORAL: Two. Yes?

ROY: Listen to me.

CORAL: The whole world is listening to you.

ROY: Just two things.

CORAL: Why don't you help me choose an evening dress to take?

ROY: I'm getting sick of this act.

CORAL: This one?

ROY: Two things. One. My position at school. I can't go on turning up at school functions with you if you're going to behave like a ghost. You wander around with that smile, staring into the distance, not seeing anyone, ignoring people.

CORAL: I don't ignore anyone.

ROY: Just let me speak. You ignore people —

CORAL: I don't.

ROY: You stare at them like there's something wrong with *them*, just stare and smile and say nothing.

CORAL: But I'm not ignoring them. I can't think of anything to say. I would never ignore anyone.

ROY: Don't split hairs, Coral. I don't care how you justify it, you behave in a way that's too . . . weird for my liking. I can feel people watching us walk away thinking, how much longer before he has to lock the poor ratbag wife up?

CORAL: People don't think like that.

ROY: Well, you're even weirder than I thought if you think like that. It has to stop. I can't keep moving school to stop you going right over the edge. There's only so much compassionate ground the Department can keep on giving me. You'll have to take stock, come back to reality.

CORAL: I mightn't like it there.

ROY: Try it for a week, for Christ's sake. Two. Second thing. I miss the boy too. I feel it. I suffer for it. Will you allow me that? Could you let me in on the sadness just a little? Because Christ I feel it.

CORAL: It's everywhere, isn't it? In the air we breathe.

ROY: But. But. We are not the only ones. We are not the first people in the history of the world to lose a son in war. There is a time for being grief stricken, there's a time for weeping and wailing and carrying on and beating your breast, but it comes to an end. It has to. Otherwise the whole world would simply stop. Jesus, Coral, in the last war practically every family lost someone or knew someone who died. They managed. They picked themselves up and went on. That's what history is, people picking themselves up, pull —ing themselves together and going on. We can't stop.

CORAL: Do you still think I look like Kim Novak?

ROY: Jesus Christ.

CORAL: You did once.

ROY: There's no point packing clothes. We won't go.

CORAL: We need a break. We need a change.

ROY: I don't need a break with you. I can stay home and read a book and be more relaxed. I'm not wasting time and money on airfare and room service if you're going to spend all your time staring at people.

CORAL: I'll be good! I'll improve. Watch me get better.

ROY: I can't take it, Coral.

CORAL: I won't think about death, about —

ROY: I'm not asking you to forget, I won't forget.

CORAL: I'll be calm, interested, aware of people. I'll look after myself. I'll get up at a proper time. I'll have fun.

ROY: You can sit by a pool all day if you like. But like a normal human being.

CORAL: We won't mention helicopters, or jungles, or mines -

ROY: I'll tear up the tickets. I'll give them away. I'll send someone else who'll enjoy it.

CORAL: I'll be silent on all controversial topics. Will that do? I won't bring up anything upsetting or worrying. Death, war, loss —

ROY: Be reasonable. Give it a rest.

CORAL: I won't blame anyone.

ROY: Please, please stop doing it to me. I didn't send him. He had to go. Would you rather not pay the price for the life we have? We could just lie down in the street, defenceless, and let whoever wanted to come and take what we have. Would that have been better for you? Would you have been happy then? Jesus, Coral, you're too selfish. We were picked out to pay. I can't help that. We've paid. I can't bring him back. So we have a duty to go on with what we have. Maybe we should even be proud? We're living in a country with one of the highest standards of living on earth and we have shown ourselves willing to defend that standard.

CORAL: Shhhh, Roy ... Shhhh, relax. We need a break. A rest. Rest and recreation. Let's get away. Just the two of us.

ROY: Coral ... be like you were.

CORAL: I will, I will.

ROY: Smile.

CORAL: I will. I'll be as good as gold. I'll be like Kim Novak. I'll purr like a kitten.

ROY: Sweetheart ...

CORAL: I don't think this dress is the right one.

ROY: Coral ...

CORAL: I know.

ROY: Look at me. *pretending*

CORAL: There.

ROY: You remind me of Kim Novak. *Vertigo?*

CORAL: You remind me ... but I mustn't say.

[*Silence.*]

We'll have a wonderful, wonderful time. *ultimate pretense death?*

SCENE FOUR

TOM *and* VIC.

VIC: I heard something. I thought we had burglars.

TOM: I was thirsty. I'm all right. I think I must be a bit

excited. I can't sleep.
VIC: I can't sleep either.
   [*Silence.*]
  Have you packed everything you need?
TOM: I don't want to take much.
VIC: It's not going to be what you'd call a flash holiday. Just the basics.
TOM: Who needs St. Tropez?
VIC: But we're going away.
TOM: And we'll have a great time.
VIC: It won't be much of a Christmas either, really. I wish I could give you a bike.
TOM: Bottle of gin'll do.
VIC: Gin?
TOM: Sure. And a handkerchief.
VIC: You've guessed it then.
TOM: I hate surprises.
VIC: Your father will enjoy this trip.
TOM: We all will.
VIC: You'll get bored. I know you. It doesn't matter if you do.
TOM: I'll have the time of my life.
VIC: But if you do get cheesed off ... try and look like you're having a real ball. You know?
TOM: I won't have to try.
VIC: You can act, we all know that now. Maybe that's what you'll end up doing with yourself.
TOM: Who knows?
VIC: Who knows? But if you could just pretend a bit ... if you have to. For your Dad.
TOM: I'll do my best.
VIC: I hope you haven't been extravagant for us.
TOM: Mink. Diamonds. A Rolls.
VIC: Well, we'll use them 'til New Year then take them back.
TOM: You look tired, Mum.
VIC: Goodnight.
   [*She goes.*]
TOM: 'Sweet friends, to bed.'

ACT THREE

SCENE ONE

A Gold Coast Luxury Hotel.
Couples in their summer best dance a spectacular pre-dinner number.
CORAL *comes in and watches them. When the music ends the others*
drift away. CORAL *approaches a woman who has found herself alone*
for a moment.

CORAL: What a way to spend Christmas Eve.
WOMAN: Isn't it lovely?
CORAL: You're a very good dancer.
WOMAN: A bit rusty.
CORAL: That's a lovely dress.
WOMAN: Thank you.
CORAL: Did you make it yourself?
WOMAN: No. Excuse me.
CORAL: Where did you buy it then?
WOMAN: In a shop. I'm looking for my husband.
CORAL: Did he buy it for you?
WOMAN:: Yes he did.
CORAL: Oh, good.
WOMAN:: Everyone's going in to dinner.
CORAL: Isn't the food here wonderful? It seems so
    extravagant. We're so lucky to be living in such a rich
    country.
WOMAN:: I suppose we are.
CORAL: There is a price that has to be paid, of course. And
    we should all be prepared to pay it. That's if we're prepared
    to enjoy this high standard of living.
WOMAN:: Yes, I'm sure.
CORAL: Have you stayed here before?
WOMAN: Every year.
CORAL: We've never been to Queensland before. We usually
    tried to all go somewhere overseas for the Christmas
    holidays. Last year we didn't. We got a house by the sea.
    I was a little worried about coming to such a big place.
    There are so many people staying here.

WOMAN: It's packed. But we like it. Excuse me, I'm getting peckish.

CORAL: And do you get on with your husband when you're on holidays.

WOMAN: Um . . . yes.

CORAL: I asked because we get so used to seeing them in the evenings for a few hours and then when we're together for a fortnight, life can get a little fraught. What's your name? I'm Coral.

WOMAN: Leonie.

CORAL: Oh, Leonie, isn't it hard making contact with other people in this kind of place? Everyone's enjoying themselves but, I don't know, I feel it's a bit forced, do you feel that? Are you really enjoying yourself? Or are you only pretending. To please your husband, perhaps?

WOMAN: [*almost in tears*] Why are you staring like that?

CORAL: If there were someone here who was in trouble would anyone know, would anyone take the trouble to find out, to try and help?

WOMAN: I'm not in any trouble.

CORAL: I'd like to be able to help someone if they were in some trouble. I mustn't go on ignoring people. Apparently I do. I've become very withdrawn. But I'm much better now. That's all over with, that part of my life is finished. I've learnt to start all over again. You have to in the end.

WOMAN: Please let me go.

CORAL: Do you have any children, Leonie?

WOMAN: No.

CORAL: Oh. Oh, well.

WOMAN: Two boys. Let me go, please, I want to go.

CORAL: Are they here with you?

WOMAN: They've gone away with some mates.

CORAL: Good. That's a good idea. Don't hang onto them.

WOMAN: Where's your husband? Does he know where you are?

CORAL: He was having a shower. I got dressed and slipped out.

WOMAN: Why don't you sit down over there? Wait for him. Over there.

CORAL: Oh, he'll be hours. Let my buy you a drink. We'll sit together and natter.

WOMAN: I can't.

CORAL: Where are you from, Leonie?

WOMAN: If you don't let me go I'll call for help.

CORAL: You are in trouble.

[*They struggle.*]

WOMAN: [*crying*] I'm not. I want to go in. I'm hungry. Let me go.

CORAL: Leonie, please. It's all right, calm down.

WOMAN: [*calling*] Frank! Frank! Help me. Please!

CORAL: What do you want to drink?

WOMAN: I want to go.

CORAL: I can see something's wrong.

[*The* WOMAN *wrenches herself free. She retreats, sobbing.*]

WOMAN: My husband has been sleeping with a twenty-year old girl. I know where she lives. I want to kill her. I'm going to have my dinner now. With my husband. Don't speak to me again. I am going to have my dinner.

[*She goes. A young man,* RICK, *has seen all this.* CORAL *stalks about unhappily for a moment then notices him.*]

RICK: I'm looking for my wife.

[*Pause.* CORAL *stares at him.*]

That woman seemed a bit upset.

[*Pause.*]

You know her?

[*Pause.*]

Did she hurt you?

CORAL: [*forcing herself to speak*] She's very unhappy.

RICK: I'd say so.

CORAL: You've lost your wife?

RICK: I think I'm in the dog house. All I wanted for lunch was hot dog. We were in the restaurant. She got a bit upset.

CORAL: Did she?

RICK: I should have had something flash. Steak Diane or something. Prawn cocktail.

CORAL: And you wanted a hot dog.

RICK: And a beer.

CORAL: Was she embarrassed?

RICK: A bit, I s'pose.

CORAL: You'd better go and have a good dinner then. Lobster Thermidor.

RICK: She said she'd be in the ballroom. Wanted to be by herself. At least I got her pressie wrapped up.

CORAL: You're on your honeymoon, aren't you?

RICK: That's right.

CORAL: I can see that.

RICK: Remind you of yours? Sorry, that wasn't very nice.

CORAL: What's your name?

RICK: Rick.

CORAL: Rick. On your honeymoon in this palace and your wife's got the huff. It's a wonderful place, isn't it? Does your room have a view?

RICK: I think so.

CORAL: [*laughing*] You haven't looked!

RICK: [*embarrassed*] Yeah, yeah, over the pool.

CORAL: I'll bet you haven't tried the pool either.

RICK: Have you?

CORAL: It's always full of kids. It's marvellous for them, though. They're so lucky to have been born in this country. We have such a high standard of living here.

RICK: Looks like it.

CORAL: There is a price that has ... [*running out of conviction*] and we all must ... you'd better hunt down your wife, Rick.

RICK: She'll turn up when she's ready.

CORAL: Go in and order some real dinner for her.

[*He starts to go then stops.*]

RICK: I think I'll wait. I don't like being in a room full of people I don't know on my own. You know any of them?

CORAL: Oh, yes, we're regulars here. I know so many people. There's a couple who are both very ill and not telling each other. Cancer, I think. Quite a few marriages on the rocks. A lot of them can't stand their own kids. And a lot of the kids hate their parents. Leonie's husband is having an affair. I know most of them, I think.

RICK: All these people.

CORAL: Quite a lot of them. We come here every year. Except last year. I wasn't the best last year. I got a bit withdrawn. I was a bit fraught. But I'm over that now. I'm much better. Much, much better.

RICK: Susie wanted to come up here. I didn't mind. But it's a bit flash for a fitter and turner. Not really the place for me.

CORAL: A fitter and turner.

RICK: Just finished me apprenticeship. I waited 'til then to get married.

CORAL: You're a sensible person.

RICK: You've got to think of the future.

CORAL: That's right.

RICK: I was scared stiff I'd get called up. I missed out being a nasho by one number. It's like a lottery, you see.

CORAL: Yes, I've heard about it.

RICK: They just pull the birthdates out of a hat, more or less. Before you know it you've won two years in the army. We all watched it on TV. Bit of a party. My month got closer and closer. I was sweating, drinking faster and faster and my day was coming up and it just missed. I nearly passed out when he called out the number after mine. Nearly fell on the floor. Two of me mates went.

CORAL: Did they?

RICK: Yep. Off to fight the Commos.

CORAL: In the jungle.

RICK: I s'pose. Christ I was scared.

CORAL: And you got married.

RICK: Yep.

CORAL: [*laughing*] Comparisons are odious.

RICK: Sorry?

CORAL: Marriage or the jungle.

RICK: Oh, right. Yeah.

CORAL: Or up in a helicopter. You see, I'm much better at communicating with others.

RICK: You are, that's for sure …

CORAL: Do I remind you of anyone?

RICK: Ahhh. Dame Pattie?

CORAL: Well —

RICK: Was that the wrong thing to say?

CORAL: No, no.

RICK: I don't know what's happened to Susie.

CORAL: You would have made a good soldier. Footslogger.

RICK: No fear.

CORAL: You'd have made it into the army very easily. You would have breezed through the medical. The uniform would have fitted you like a glove. Your hair might have needed a bit of a trim.

RICK: Bit of a Beatle.

CORAL: It's a wonderful colour. So thick.

RICK: I like her a lot. I've known her since school. She was very keen to get married. She's really nice. You'd like her. She's a bit shy, but. When we've saved up for a house we might think about kids. 'Til then.

[ROY *rushes in, his jacket half on. He stops and gets his breath.*]

ROY: I wondered where you'd got to.

CORAL: Rick's on his honeymoon.

ROY: Congratulations, son. [*To* CORAL] I told you to wait for me.

CORAL: I've been having a terrific time. We've been talking about the standard of living in this country.

ROY: They're serving dinner.

CORAL: We can't leave Rick.

RICK: I'll wait for Susie.

CORAL: Sit with us when you come in.

ROY: [*leading her away*] He's on his honeymoon, darling. Let him sit where he likes.

CORAL: [*to* ROY] I'm doing well, aren't I? I've started taking such an interest in the world around me. Have a lovely Christmas morning, Rick.

[RICK *watches them go, checks his watch and waits for his wife.*]

SCENE TWO

A tent and caravan city.
GWEN *carries a twelve-inch fake Christmas tree.*

GWEN: If you want to have a Christmas you'd better get started now so we can get it over with. Hurry up. I don't intend spending half the day sitting around waiting for people to open their presents.

[MEG *enters*.]

Everyone else has been up for hours and got the thing over with. Look, they're all down on the beach already. Most of the boats have gone out. There'll be no fish left out there for us. [*Calling*] You kids there! Get those bikes away from the tent ropes! Go on! You'll fall off! You'll end up with a tent peg through your skull! Won't be much of a Christmas then, will it?. Go on! [*Back to* MEG] Why would you give a kiddy a bike in a camping ground? They should think about what they give their children for Christmas. And the salt water'll rust them in a week. And on Christmas morning you can't walk to the shower block without being mown down by a whole pack of scooters and bikes.

[JIM *enters*.]

JIM: Has anyone seen a little carton?

GWEN: No.

JIM: A cardboard carton about so big.

GWEN: What carton?

JIM: One of those cartons you bring home from the supermarket. I kept it from going out in the garbage.

GWEN: I haven't seen it.

JIM: Not when we unpacked?

GWEN: No.

JIM: It must be somewhere.

GWEN: What do you need a cardboard carton for?

MEG: What was in it?

JIM: Oh … something.

GWEN: You packed the car.

JIM: I was sure I left it with the cases.

GWEN: Well, I didn't see any cartons, cardboard or otherwise.

JIM: Don't tell me it didn't come with us. It can't have been left behind.

GWEN: Well, what was in it that was so important?

JIM: You sure you haven't seen it?

GWEN: Do you want to search the place?

JIM: It must have come. Oh, no.

MEG: What was in it?

JIM: All my presents for you. I hid them in a little carton and
put it with all the other stuff so you wouldn't notice it.

GWEN: Oh, well, it looks like you hid them a bit too well.
That's a shame. Well, we may as well have what's left of
Christmas anyway. Margaret, Merry Christmas. These are
the books you'll need. This one's underwear. Jim, there
are your socks. That's your fishing reel. I hope its the one
you asked for. Merry Christmas.

JIM: I can't believe it. How did it happen? I'm sorry.

GWEN: Now don't throw the wrapping paper everywhere. I'm
not spending the day chasing wrapping paper all over the
State. Though it doesn't look like there'll be much this year.

JIM: I hid them in a cardboard box. I left it with the suitcases
so it would just get packed, no questions asked, and you
wouldn't suspect and look inside.

GWEN: That backfired. And we go without Christmas. [*To*
MEG] Are you going to hand yours over? Or can I go and
start lunch?

MEG: Here you are. Merry Christmas.

GWEN: Thanks. Are these the …?

MEG: Yes, the plastic mugs.

GWEN: Marvellous. Thank you. I won't unwrap them all
here. And what did you get?

JIM: Just a little cardboard box.

GWEN: I think your needle's stuck. What have you got?

MEG: It's that fishing book.

GWEN: Oh, that's nice.

JIM: So big it was.

GWEN: I'm not going to stand here nattering.

MEG: I saw the carton.

JIM: Don't worry, it doesn't matter.

MEG: I saw it in the hall.

JIM: Drop it, sweetheart.

MEG: I saw it. It was near the telephone table, wasn't it?

JIM: That's right but it doesn't matter now.

GWEN: Christmas is only for the young ones, anyway. I don't
know why we bother any more.

JIM: I was just so sure it would get packed.

GWEN: I can start cutting up the vegies, I suppose.

MEG: You saw it too, didn't you? You saw the box sitting there.

GWEN: I did no such thing.

MEG: You must have. It was sitting next to your vanity case.

GWEN: I didn't see any cardboard carton.

MEG: Everything else that was in the hall got packed in the car. You did see it.

GWEN: Don't argue with me.

MEG: You were the last one out. You're the one who shuts the door, after you've made sure the stove's off and the fridge has been left open. You saw the carton and you left it there on purpose.

GWEN: I most certainly did not.

MEG: You left it behind

JIM: I'll make it up. I'll take us all to the pub for lunch.

GWEN: You won't get me into that stinking pub.

MEG: And you knew what it was. You knew what was in it and you left it there.

GWEN: I will not be accused outside my own caravan. On Christmas morning.

MEG: Why did you do that?

GWEN: I'm not on trial.

MEG: Why would you do a thing like that?

JIM: Well, it's done now. What's done is done.

MEG: I want to know why you did it.

GWEN: You watch your tongue, my girl.

MEG: Tell me why you deliberately left that box behind.

JIM: Don't speak to your mother like that.

MEG: We have a game we play every year. We sneak presents home, we hide them, we wrap them up in secret even though we can hear the sticky tape tearing and the paper rustling; we hide them in the stuff we take away, we pretend not to see them until Christmas morning even when we know they're there and we know what's in them because we've already put in our orders so there's no waste or surprise. And Dad always hides his in a pathetic place that's so obvious it's a joke and we all laugh at him behind our

backs but we play along! You knew what was in that box.
You left it behind. I want to know why.

GWEN: Where have you picked up these ugly manners?

MEG: What were you trying to do, what did you want to gain?

JIM: It's only old presents. Slippers and your new bread knife.

MEG: Did you want to have something we'd all have to be
sorry for the whole holiday? There's always something we
do wrong that takes you weeks to forgive.

GWEN: Where did you learn to say all this?

MEG: You have to tell me.

GWEN: The things that are taken away on holidays always go
in the proper order, so everything will fit. I can't help it
if someone decides to be smart and funny and try to hide
things in a little cardboard box. I wasn't going to have the
whole routine upset, that we've been following all these
years and that I thought was giving people a good life,
though it seems I'm very wrong, for the sake of someone's
joke.

MEG: But to do it deliberately!

GWEN: You're developing a nasty streak. A very nasty, cruel
streak. You know what you're becoming? Snide. A nasty,
snide girl. No one likes a snide girl, always arguing, always
throwing a tantrum, getting your own way, answering back,
correcting people, criticising, complaining, no one likes that
sort of girl. Unless you count your foulmouthed little
English chum. You'll make a great pair. Throw your future
away. Give it away. Throw what I have done, we have
done, in our faces.

MEG: What have you done?

JIM: Let's all calm down.

GWEN: Sacrificed! Gone without. Gone through hardship so
what happened to us will never happen to you. So you'll
never know what we saw — never, never, never. Never
see people losing jobs and never finding another one, never
be without a home, never be without enough money for
a decent meal, never be afraid that everything will fall apart
at any second. Isn't that something, miss? Tell me? Isn't it?

JIM: Let's all relax and calm down.

MEG: I'm sorry.

JIM: Just sit down, nice and quiet.

MEG: I'm sorry.

GWEN: Why are you so cruel?

MEG: I'm sorry.

GWEN: Now my head's going to burst. I'm going to take
something and then get lunch.
        [*She goes.*]

JIM: I asked you. I begged you.

MEG: I couldn't help myself.

JIM: What good could it do? What do you want her to do
now, after all this time?

MEG: Smile.
        [*Pause.*]

JIM: When we were first courting I took her to the pictures
to see *Gone With the Wind*. Afterwards she was so quiet, but
excited, something in her head was turning over and over.
She was living in this funny little house in Surry Hills then,
with all her sisters, it was a pretty dirty area. The next week
I went round to take her out to a dance.

Everyone else had gone on some church picnic and she was
home on her own so I knew we'd have a few minutes alone.
I got there a bit early because I couldn't think of anything
else I'd rather be doing. I went round the back and as I
went past the kitchen window I could hear her talking to
someone. I stopped at the back door. She was saying what
old Vivien Leigh said in *Gone With the Wind* — just before
the intermission and the war's been on and everyone's dead
and the house's wrecked and the crops burnt and she's
scratching around in the dirt for some old potato or cotton
or something just to feed her family and she stands up
against that red sky and says: 'As God is my witness, I
will never be hungry again.' I laughed, not at her but I
was really bowled over, she was as good as old Vivien any
day. She was very embarrassed and so was I and we made
a bit of a joke of it. But seeing her upset before made me
remember that afternoon. 'I will never be hungry again.'
It had that effect on a lot of people, that film. Old Scarlet
standing in that field and wanting to rule the world.
        [*A clump of* CAMPERS *comes in.*]

ALL: Merry Christmas!

JIM: And you

SECOND CAMPER: Having a good time this year?

JIM: Can't complain.

FOURTH CAMPER: Not so close to the water this year.

JIM: No, we were beaten to it.

ALL: A lot of us were.

THIRD CAMPER: Not one regular got a spot close to the water this summer.

JIM: Oh, well.

FIRST CAMPER: We've been talking to a few people.

THIRD CAMPER: Going around the whole site, actually.

FIRST CAMPER: Just saying —

FOURTH CAMPER: Merry Christmas.

THIRD CAMPER: And having a quiet word with the more or less regular campers and caravanners.

FOURTH CAMPER: We've even thought of getting up a bit of a petition.

FIRST CAMPER: But that might be a bit drastic to start with.

SECOND CAMPER: So we're just having a quiet word first.

THIRD CAMPER: To test the water, so to speak.

FIRST CAMPER: I'm a Rotary man myself and I'm used to a bit of —

ALL: Organising!

FIRST CAMPER: So I started mentioning a few, what you might call, grievances.

THIRD CAMPER: ⎫
FOURTH CAMPER: ⎬ Not major grievances.

FIRST CAMPER: But grievances just the same that we — the ordinary regular camper, is experiencing.

SECOND CAMPER: And since you've been coming here as long as anyone we felt it important to include you in this initial group.

FIRST CAMPER: With your lady wife as well.

JIM: I don't have any grievances.

FOURTH CAMPER: A spot so far from the water, for example!

JIM: Luck of the draw, first in first —

THIRD CAMPER: But mightn't you feel that as a camper of many years standing you might expect a spot closer to the water?

SECOND CAMPER: As opposed to someone, say, who happened to turn off the highway taking *pot luck*?

JIM: Like I said, first in —

FIRST CAMPER: We've been considering an idea of somehow assuring regular campers a better deal.

ALL: A priority system.

FIRST CAMPER: Of reserving spots by the water.

ALL: The longer you've been coming here the closer to the water.

FIRST CAMPER: And there's the shower and toilet block. It needs expanding.

SECOND CAMPER:
FOURTH CAMPER: } It isn't coping at all.

FIRST CAMPER: We were thinking of approaching Council to build us a proper brick and cement structure. Toilets, showers and a small shop selling essentials, hot food.

THIRD CAMPER: Beachy things.

SECOND CAMPER:
FOURTH CAMPER: } You know.

FIRST CAMPER: Also laundry facilities.

FOURTH CAMPER: And a large kitchen area.

FIRST CAMPER: For when those women folk really feel the need to cook up a storm.

THIRD CAMPER: They should feel right at home while they're on holiday.

SECOND CAMPER: } Something a bit smarter than the old
FOURTH CAMPER: } primus.

FIRST CAMPER: We're also a little concerned about some of the people who've started putting in an appearance over the last few years.

SECOND CAMPER:
FOURTH CAMPER: } Drifter types.

THIRD CAMPER: Not proper families.

FIRST CAMPER: And some of the New Australian campers might need to be reminded of the way proper Australian families run a holiday.

SECOND CAMPER: } They're not bobbing around in the
FOURTH CAMPER: } Mediterranean now.

FIRST CAMPER: There's also a beautification plan under way. We want to remove —

ALL: All those trees!

FIRST CAMPER: They pose a serious threat in any sort of wind.

SECOND CAMPER: A branch from one of those could put a nasty hole in your caravan.

FOURTH CAMPER: And the kiddies are always as risk from —

SECOND CAMPER: } Ticks.
FOURTH CAMPER:

FIRST CAMPER: We think there should be some sort of caretaker too, to look after the grass. Also we'd like to see some solid steps down onto the beach, with handrails, to make the beach more accessible to everyone.

THIRD CAMPER: A carparking area right down on the rock platform would be a good idea too.

SECOND CAMPER: And there's been a lot of concern about the building of the lookout.

FIRST CAMPER: If we're going to turn that headland into a scenic attraction we're going to have to do a lot of work —

ALL: To make it work!

THIRD CAMPER: There needs to be a gravel surface road up to the lookout itself.

FIRST CAMPER: As well as a decent turning circle —

SECOND CAMPER: } and a cyclone wire fence to make it
FOURTH CAMPER: } perfectly safe.

THIRD CAMPER: We've got a list here of our proposals as well as a few other ideas.

FIRST CAMPER: Draining the lagoon,

SECOND CAMPER: Banning pets,

FOURTH CAMPER: And keeping the under twenties —

ALL: out of the Saturday night dances!

FIRST CAMPER: We'll leave one with you.

SECOND CAMPER: See what you think.

THIRD CAMPER: There'll be a public meeting in the Hall the day after New Year's day.

JIM: Thank you.

SECOND CAMPER: Have a lovely Christmas Day.

FOURTH CAMPER: Big lunch on the way?

JIM: I . . . I'd say so.

[*They all howl with laughter and go. Silence.*]

MEG: I got a tick once. You said it would burrow through to my brain.

JIM: There was no one here that year except a few abalone divers.

MEG: And they went swimming in the nuddy. And Mum hit the roof.

JIM: Went after them with a broom.

[*He folds up the list, looks at it and tears it into pieces.*]

SCENE THREE

The roof of the Gold Coast Hotel.
    CORAL *and* RICK.

CORAL: I found myself up here by accident.

RICK: As long as we're not away too long.

CORAL: I got out of the lift on the wrong floor and saw a door.

RICK: A few people saw us sneak out.

CORAL: I thought, why not? It said no entry but they didn't mean me.

RICK: I don't care what they might think.

CORAL: I came up those stairs and here I was on the roof.

RICK: Some of them like making snide remarks. Susie might get the wrong idea.

CORAL: There! Now look at the view. Aren't you sorry I got you away from that party? You can see the mountains.

RICK: Susie's a little bit suspicious, I think. I'm always just going to meet you when she wants to do something.

CORAL: And you can see the whole of the town.

RICK: She seems to know just when I'm going to see you. Maybe I get nervous and she can tell. Do I get nervous?

CORAL: It's even better up here at night. With this breeze.

RICK: Do I get nervous?

CORAL: It's like a desert in the daytime.

RICK: I want to know if I'm acting nervous whenever I meet you.

CORAL: No, of course not.

RICK: I don't want Susie to think I'm up to anything wrong. I am on my honeymoon.

CORAL: Wrong?

RICK: But I get excited when I know it's time to see you again.

CORAL: We like each other.

RICK: But I get excited.

CORAL: Look at the lights. And the cars.

RICK: And maybe she can sense that because then she sulks and gets really moody and won't talk to me. I make an excuse to get out and then I see you and we go somewhere and all we do is talk.

CORAL: I like to talk.

RICK: Then when I go back she wants to go out and I don't. I just feel like sitting and drinking. She gets upset and sulks again. I should tell her where I'm going.

CORAL: She'd hate that.

RICK: I don't understand her. But I'm married to her.

CORAL: You're on your honeymoon.

RICK: And if I try to make it up to her and be close when I touch her she rips her arm away and goes down to the shops or orders some food. She won't look at me.

CORAL: Rick, don't worry about that.

RICK: Then the phone rings and there's no one there. I know it's you and that makes me nervous. I bet she knows!

CORAL: But we're here on our own.

RICK: And you pass messages to me and when I read them I want to walk away from whatever I'm doing and talk to you straight away. She can tell, I know she can. We won't talk to each other any more.

CORAL: Why not?

RICK: It's the wrong thing to do. I'm on my honeymoon. I've known her since school.

CORAL: You can't stop being with me.

RICK: We'll pack up and go somewhere else. What if her family found out? How would that look? I don't understand why I do this. Why do you want to see me?

CORAL: You're still alive. You're still alive and talking and laughing.

RICK: I'm just going round the twist, I think. I do things I don't understand. I have a job I didn't want. I got married and I can't remember why. I'm going to buy a house and I can't remember why. I spend all day waiting to talk to this woman I don't know. I'm going to end up in a straight-jacket. Everything I do is wrong. But I can't help myself. I just do things and I don't see why.

CORAL: Come into the dark. Over here. Come over here. Give me your hand.

RICK: I feel like I'm asleep all the time.

CORAL: Come into the shadows. A boy like you . . .

[*They disappear into the dark.*]

RICK: Like in a dream.

CORAL: Here in the corner. In the dark. A boy like you . . . talk . . . talk to me . . . say something . . . laugh . . .

[*Silence for a moment.* ROY *comes onto the roof. He paces around, searching.*]

ROY: Coral? Sweetheart? Come back to the party. Why did you run out? Come back to the party. Where are you? I followed you. I had to. I love you. Don't hide away like this. Don't hide from me. I brought you a drink. To celebrate. To toast the New Year. A better year. This one'll be a better year all round. We'll make it a better year. No looking back.

[*In the distance we hear cheering, singing of 'Auld Lang Syne', car horns.*]

There it is. You'll miss it, quick. Nineteen sixty-eight.

CORAL: Here we are. We're here.

RICK: Where are you going?

CORAL: We're here. Happy New Year! Happy New Year!

[CORAL *and* RICK *come out of the dark.*]

We were hiding. Here we are. You've only got two glasses. That's all right. We'll share. Happy New Year! Drink from the glass with me. Here you are.

[RICK *takes the glass.*]

CORAL: We're all here together. Look at that sky. There's a storm down south. Watch for the lightning.

ROY: Straighten yourself up, boy.

CORAL: Don't nag.

ROY: Somebody's probably looking for you.

    [RICK *goes*.]

What am I going to do with you?

CORAL: You sent him away.

ROY: I'm going to have to do something. See someone.

CORAL: [*a great cry*] You sent him away!

ROY: Do you want me to send you to a doctor? Do you want to see a doctor? Do you want me to arrange shock treatment? I can. I looked into it. It's very easy. I just have to take you to a doctor and they plug you in and that's that. Look at you. Look at me. I'll lock you up if that's what it takes. I'll keep you under lock and key if you insist. But you won't behave like this. You won't ever see another living person. You won't bother anyone. You won't see another living person. I'll look after you. I'll come and visit you.

CORAL: Don't worry about me. You don't have to worry about me. I'm going down to our room and I'll have a good think about what you said. I'll sort things out. Give me the key, darling. Is it in this pocket? Give me a little while. I'll be as right as rain. [*Leaving*] I'll gather my thoughts and turn things over and over in my mind. I'll weigh things up and come to a decision. But don't worry about me I'll be fine.

    [ROY *leans out over the parapet and listens to the sound of the party*.]

SCENE FOUR

Storm scene.

    The FAIRIES *return and stage a spectacular storm, emptying the stage to the sound of Mendelssohn's Wedding March.*

JIM: Put the clothes in the car.

GWEN: Take the stove!

JIM: I'm going to try and dig a trench.

GWEN: You'll get struck by lightning.

JIM: Stay in the car.

GWEN: Where's my purse?
JIM: Stay in the open.
GWEN: The boat will be washed away.
JIM: Stay away from the trees.
[JIM, GWEN *and* MEG *are driven out by the* FAIRIES, *who wreak havoc with noise, light and frenzied activity.*]

SCENE FIVE

As the storm subsides there is darkness. The opening bars of Mendelssohn's Dream *overture are heard. The light becomes warm and intense.* TOM, VIC *and* HARRY *are discovered on a beach. She is wearing a spectacular sunhat,* HARRY *has a fishing reel.* TOM *is wearing board shorts and an Hawaiian shirt.*

VIC: Where will we go today?
TOM: Round onto the rocks?
HARRY: What about going round to the next beach?
VIC: We've got enough food.
HARRY: The next beach?
TOM: The next beach it is.
VIC: We were lucky to miss that storm.
HARRY: We were very lucky.
VIC: I'll bet it did some damage.
HARRY: We'd have been all right. We could have sheltered under your hat.
VIC: I love my new hat.
HARRY: We all did well out of Santa. New hat, new reel, new bathers.
VIC: Don't get too burnt.
TOM: I'll be fine.
VIC: Let's go round to the next beach, then.
[*They go.*]

ACT FOUR

SCENE ONE

The beach.
   VIC, HARRY, JIM *and* GWEN.

VIC: The headland shelters the beach from the wind. You can
   sit round there under the rocks on the coolest day and be
   as hot as chips. There's a rockpool over there that's almost
   a perfect rectangle. You'd think it had been carved out by
   human hands. The bottom's covered in sand. Even I go
   in it and I'm terrified of what might be hiding in most
   rockpools. At the other end there's a cave that you can get
   into at low tide. It goes right in under that dairy on the
   hill, the one you drove past on the way in here. There's
   a track from the cave right up the cliff onto the headland.
   At night up there you can see the lights of the town, way,
   way over there and the lighthouse on the island. And past
   that headland there's a beach that must be, oh, five — ?
HARRY: Five at least, seven —
VIC: Yes, seven miles long without a break. We walk around
   there for a picnic. You get halfway along and look back
   and there are just three lines of footprints trailing away into
   the distance. It's marvellous to sit in the middle of that
   beach, the three of us. Sometimes when it's really hot it's
   nice to slip your bathers off in the water and just swim about
   like a fish.
JIM: It is a lovely spot, isn't it?
   [GWEN *nods unwillingly.*]
HARRY: And at the end of that beach there's a headland, a
   big rock platform. In the middle there's a carving in the
   rock. A man with a spear. And a big kangaroo. How old
   did that fellow say it was?
VIC: Five thousand years. At least.
HARRY: Five thousand years!
VIC: It is a wonderful place. And what a piece of luck you
   found it.

JIM: It was just chance, wasn't it?

> [GWEN *nods again.*]

After that storm we salvaged what we could and dried it out. We thought we'd just go straight home. There didn't seem much point in carrying on after that washout. There doesn't seem to be a reason to carry on with your holiday when your van's a wreck, your boat's smashed on the rocks and all your clothes are soaked. But we tried to save something of the holiday and spent a few nights in this motel. It was a funny place. Run by this old cheese who wore thongs all the time. They were old thongs, very loose and you could hear her, flap, flap, flap, coming down the passageway. They'd stop for a second, then start again. I suppose she was listening at a door. I don't know what she thought people might be up to, the rooms were really tiny. We stuck it out for a couple of nights. But ... we didn't enjoy it. It wasn't our sort of place. So we decided to head for home. We drove all day yesterday and we were getting pretty hot and tired and the girl suddenly pointed at a road sign and said we had to turn off the highway. She really wanted us to, kept insisting. So I turned the car around and drove back to the road sign and turned off down the dirt road. And when we came up over the last hill and saw the beach ...

HARRY: Yes, you were very lucky.

VIC: And you got here in time for the campers' amateur night. It's how we end our holidays. It's a great night. You'll laugh till you're sick.

HARRY: It's a great way to end a holiday.

VIC: And it's been a wonderful holiday this year.

> [CORAL *enters in a flowing kaftan, dark glasses a huge straw hat over a scarf.*]

Look, there she is, the artist.

> [*She waves.* CORAL *goes out without seeing them.*]

Isn't she an interesting looking woman? She's been here a few days now. She just arrived one morning, all by herself. I think she might be an artist or something, so that's what I call her. She goes and sits on the rock ledge for hours and stares into the sea. She keeps to herself, right away from everyone. The world is full of interesting people.

GWEN: [*violently*] The world is full of mad people. Everywhere, mad people. Why do they have to live like that? Mad people, weird, sick, sordid people. How do they bear having no worthwhile aim? I'm tired to people who don't want to improve. I'm sick to death of people who are happy to just stay in the mud, in the swamp, just thrashing about, who don't try for a better life, to fight their way out with their bare hands. I hate them — they're happy in their filthy little holes like that motel — that was a nightmare! — I hate them. They're everywhere. Like ants, swarming everywhere, no direction, no ambition —

    [*She stifles herself. Silence.*]

VIC: I think we should go for a walk.

GWEN: No.

VIC: Us girls. Along the water.

GWEN: No.

VIC: Just a stroll. Come on.

JIM: Go on. Breathe some sea air.

    [*The women go. Silence for a while.*]

HARRY: Yes, you were lucky.

JIM: It was the girl's idea completely. She . . . my wife, gave up. She was very upset. But the girl kept on at me. She didn't let up until we were on that dirt road. She's a handful.

    [*Pause.*]

HARRY: This is a wonderful country. We're still not used to a hot Christmas.

JIM: My wife is not really an angry woman. She has high hopes.

HARRY: We have no regrets. We don't get homesick. Only once a year. We book a telephone call to our old street. In Nottingham. We get out the photo album. Remember for a while. But we have no regrets. This country ... and often when we do think back, all we can think of is the cold, the tiny houses, the rationing, the rubble after the war. It was a rubbish dump. A lot wanted to stay and help to build again. But we didn't want to. We felt held back. We knew why the sailors had called it the Old World. It was like living with an elderly relative, tired, cranky, who doesn't want

you to have any fun but just worry about their health all
the time. Nagging you, criticising you, making you feel
guilty for any enjoyment you might manage to find. No
regrets. In a funny kind of way we're happy. Even while
we're very, very sad. We have no regrets, but we have no
hopes. Not any more. We might get some, but it's unlikely,
I think. Our son is very sick. It's a cancer of the blood.
He was very bad this year, we thought it was time to get
ready. But he got through it. It's called 'in remission'. But
it will come back. Every day we watch for bruises. Or to
see if he's more tired than usual. We made it into another
year at least. But we don't look forward. We haven't given
up, no, no. That would be a mistake. We don't look back
and we don't look forward. We have this boy and we won't
have him for long. And whatever he does, that will have
to be enough. The Chinese don't believe in being too upset
when someone dies. That would mean you thought they'd
died too soon and what they'd done up till then didn't
amount to much. We will be sad, of course.

[*Silence.*]

JIM: I can't think of anything to say.

HARRY: Don't ever say anything about it. Ever. Give me
your word.

JIM: I won't.

HARRY: He doesn't know. He won't know. We mustn't let
him know. He must not be afraid. He must never suspect.
He must look ahead even if we never do. Understand?

JIM: I promise.

HARRY: We don't tell most people. Very occasionally we run
into someone who needs to know. But we don't tell very
many. Did you manage to save your fishing gear?

JIM: A few reels. The rods were broken or washed away.

HARRY: What a pity.

[*The women come back. They have been crying and are supporting
each other.*]

VIC: Here she is. I brought her back. The water's very warm
today. We had a quick paddle.

[*Silence for a moment. They all look at each other.*]

HARRY: The boy wants some things in town for the show

tonight. We'd better make tracks.

VIC: Come to the concert.

HARRY: Of course they will.

VIC: You'll have a wonderful night.

HARRY: They'll be there, won't you?

JIM: We'll be there.

[VIC *and* HARRY *go. Silence.*]

GWEN: If you want to ask me what I think or how I feel . . .
I couldn't say.

JIM: I can guess.

GWEN: What do you think of me? You must hate me? Why
do you still bother? I'm sorry . . . there are all these
questions I want to ask. And not just you. Everybody.

JIM: Do you want to head off?

GWEN: Go home? No.

JIM: Do you feel all right?

GWEN: I feel . . . give me a drink.

[*He gets her one.*]
I feel . . . no, I can't say, I can't tell you. Those two people
. . . what am I trying to say?

JIM: Here's your drink. Is your head aching?

GWEN: I'm not sure. What am I trying to say?

JIM: Don't worry yourself.

GWEN: I have to. I have to worry myself. What is it I'm trying
to say?

JIM: You're over-tired.

GWEN: Don't protect me. Tell me what I'm feeling.

JIM: Shocked?

GWEN: Yes . . .

JIM: Amazed, sad?

GWEN: Not those things. They're so weak.

JIM: The girl would know. She'd hit the nail on the head.

[*She tries to take a Bex powder.*]

GWEN: I can't take this powder. I can't make it go in. I want
to take it and it won't go in. I'm going to be sick.

JIM: Give it to me.

GWEN: There's a terrible taste in my mouth.

JIM: I'll get rid of it. Relax.

GWEN: I'm sorry.

JIM: You should lie down.

GWEN: No. Let's walk. Come on, down to the water. The water's so warm.

[*They go.*]

SCENE TWO

TOM *and* MEG.

TOM: Give up?

MEG: Not yet.

TOM: You won't guess.

MEG: I've seen her before.

TOM: Come on, give up.

MEG: No I've seen her. I know her.

TOM: Then who is she?

MEG: Don't tell me. I give up.

TOM: You give up?

MEG: Yes.

TOM: You can't think who she is?

MEG: I give up.

TOM: Our headmaster's wife.

MEG: Headmaster?

TOM: That's right.

MEG: No.

TOM: Yes it is.

MEG: That's incredible.

TOM: I knew who she was the second I saw her. No one else knows. She's a very good actress.

MEG: The headmaster's wife.

TOM: That's right. She's run away. She left him in this luxury hotel on New Year's Eve. Can you believe it? She hitched here.

MEG: Hitchhiked. And dressed like that?

TOM: Dressed like that.

MEG: Your parents don't recognise her?

TOM: No. I knew, though. I went straight up to her and wished her a Happy New Year. I called her name and she turned around. I called out, 'Gotcha' and she laughed. She told me the whole story. We're great friends. She ran away from him because he was going to have her put away.

MEG: Is she crazy?

TOM: She has been. She's better now.

MEG: Really mad?

TOM: Not any more. She's been talking to people she said. She doesn't feel any different to anyone else any more. I told her … well, I told her a thing or two that helped. She's ready to get back into the swim, she says.

MEG: But she's not a real lunatic.

TOM: She might have been for a minute or two.

MEG: And she's in disguise.

TOM: That's right.

MEG: She looks like a film star.

TOM: Kim Novak.

MEG: Does she?

TOM: Yeah, I picked it straight off.

MEG: Kim Novak?

TOM: What do you think of our beach?

MEG: It's fantastic. We had a terrible argument before we came here. Mum just wanted to get back to the Pino-clean and Rinso. I kept nagging. I was being a real pain in the neck. But it would have been such a waste. We would have spent months in misery just getting over it. I wanted us to take a chance for once and see what was here.

TOM: Good on you. Do you want to sit down?

MEG: Aren't we walking to the headland?

TOM: Eventually. Sit down.

[*Pause.*]

MEG: Ummm. No. Let's keep walking.

TOM: Let's sunbake for a while.

MEG: I don't have a costume.

TOM: Don't need one.

MEG: No.

TOM: What's the problem?

MEG: Now look —

TOM: Come on —

MEG: You're frightening me.

TOM: I'm not.

MEG: All of a sudden I'm scared.

TOM: Come on —

MEG: I'm afraid.

TOM: Bull!

MEG: Please.

TOM: Lie down.

MEG: Why did you lead me here?

TOM: Lie down here.

MEG: Don't be like this.

TOM: I said lie down.

MEG: No.

TOM: Come here!

MEG: I can scream really well.

TOM: I want you to let me do it to you.

MEG: Let you? I don't want to.

TOM: Please.

MEG: No.

TOM: You have to.

MEG: I'm going to scream.

TOM: All right, I'm in love with you.

MEG: No you're not.

TOM: I want to. I have to, Please, please. Just once. Oh
Christ, please. Come on. Just lie down. I won't hurt you.
I have to.

MEG: Why are you crying?

TOM: Don't say no. Do you want me to beg?

MEG: No.

TOM: I will. Please, I beg you.

MEG: Stop it, get up. What's the matter? Maybe you're
cracked as well, maybe it's catching.

TOM: What will make you give in? What can I say?

MEG: Nothing.

TOM: What can I do?

MEG: Nothing, nothing.

TOM: I want to do it once, just once.

MEG: You will.

TOM: You remember when I missed school this year?

MEG: Yes, you were away for months.

TOM: Where was I?

MEG: You were sick.

TOM: But where was I?

MEG: You were in hospital for a while.

TOM: For a long while. What was wrong with me?

MEG: You had some infection.

TOM: Yeah, that's what I had. An infection. Everyone knew I had some infection. I was sick. I was told the infection was running its course. That I had to fight. I did. One day a doctor came and sat on my bed and had a long talk with me. He told me that before I got completely well again I would get a lot worse, get really, really sick. And no matter how sick I got not to worry because it meant that soon I'd start to get well again. He was full of shit. He couldn't look me in the face to say it. He stared at the cabinet next to the bed the whole time. And the nurses were really happy whenever they were near me, but when I stared them in the face, in the end they'd look away and bite their lips. When I was able to go home the doctor took me into his office and we had another talk. I had to look after myself. No strain, no dangerous activity. Keep my spirits up. Then he went very quiet, leant over the desk, practically whispering how if I knew a girl it'd be good for me to do it, to try it. 'It', he kept calling it. It, it. I put him on the spot. What? Name it. Give it a name. He cleared his throat. 'Sexual intercourse'. But if I was worried about going all the way I could experiment with mutual masturbation. Know what that is?

MEG: I think it's pretty clear.

TOM: I nearly spat in his face. You shocked?

MEG: I don't know.

TOM: So how about it? Help me. I'm going to get sick again. And I won't get better. Your parents won't find out.

MEG: Will yours?

TOM: They don't know. That I know. They want me to think I'm going to be as right as rain. They mustn't find out I know. They mustn't even suspect, the poor bastards. And you won't fill them in.

MEG: OK.

TOM: Will you?

MEG: OK.

TOM: No, come on.

MEG: I give you my word.

TOM: Do you?

MEG: You have my word.

TOM: Now ... what do you say?

MEG: I can't.
   [*Silence.*]
 I'm sorry.

TOM: I'm a real creep, aren't I?

MEG: It's just that ... well ... you're a bit skinny for me.
   [*Pause.*]

TOM: I could build myself up.

MEG: Well ...

TOM: Yes. I could build myself up. Do a Charles Atlas
course. Would that help?

MEG: It might.

TOM: I'll do it.

MEG: Are you really as sick as that?

TOM: Not today, not today.

MEG: If you could have seen your face before. Are you afraid?

TOM: You coming to the concert tonight?

MEG: Will I get in?

TOM: Front row. You won't let them find out, will you?

MEG: I swear.

TOM: Go on then, swear.

MEG: Oh ... blast! I'll see you at the concert.
   [*She goes.*]

TOM: Hey!
   [*She stops. He starts to do push ups, laughing. She watches him.
   When he looks up again she's gone. He lies on his back and covers
   his face with his hands, lies there for a moment.* CORAL *comes
   in with an armful of wood.*]

CORAL: Will this be enough?

TOM: For kindling.

CORAL: Oh. I'm not a pyromaniac, so I wasn't sure how
much you'll need.

TOM: Come on, we'll make a real effort. Then you've got
lines to learn.

CORAL: I'll bet Kim Novak has more than an afternoon to

get into a part. You're not feeling . . . sick or anything?
Tired?

TOM: No. Come on.
[*They go.*]

SCENE THREE

The amateur night. MC *appears in a spot. He is dressed as a hula
girl. He is carrying a ukelele.*

MC: What did Tarzan say when he saw the elephants coming?
Eh? 'Here come the elephants!' How do you fit four
elephants in a Mini Minor? Easy. Two in the front and
two in the back. Here's a trick one. What did Tarzan say
when he saw the elephants coming with sunglasses on?
VIC: 'Here come the elephants!'
MC: No, he didn't say anything 'cos he didn't recognise
them. Ha ha ha. Now — why did the elephants cross the
road? Give up? It was the chook's day off. Ha ha ha.
[*He begins to play the ukelele.*]

> Pearly shells, by the ocean,
> Lying in the sun, covering the shore.
> When I see them, my heart tells me that I love you
> More than all those little pearly shells.
>
> For every grain of sand upon the shore
> I've got a kiss for you.
> And I've got more left over than each star
> That twinkles in the blue.
>
> Pearly shells, by the ocean etc.

Don't applaud just throw money, ha ha ha. Now to round
off the concert tonight we've got something a little different
from what we usually have, but one year without hokey
pokey won't kill you, will it? Will it?
ALL: Noooo.
MC: And Alice Macfaddyn had that nasty tussle with the blue-
bottle so she's not up to singing 'Vilia' for us, so settle back,

relax, kick off your shoes as two of our fellow holidaymakers present a heart warming drama they've knocked
together themselves entitled *The Stranger on the Shore*. OK,
kids.

[TOM *appears before the curtain. He is wearing a sailor's cap.*]

TOM: There was once this sailor who was watching the stars
one night, a few miles off the Cape of Good Hope. He'd
had too much rum that night and he lost his balance. 'I'm
falling, I'm falling. What is this cold wetness that envelopes
me? It is the sea. I can see my life flashing past my eyes.
I'm drowning, I'm drowning. Down I go. To the bottom.'
So he drowned. And when he got to heaven he was so piss
... drunk they wouldn't let him in. He was turned away
at the door. 'Now I shall have to wander the high seas
forever and forever roam the docks until I atone. Endless
torture.' One night as he was wandering around the port
of Rotterdam —

[CORAL *makes ship noises on a bottle.*]

... he met this strange woman.

[CORAL's *leg appears through the curtain, then her face.*]

CORAL: [*with American accent*] 'Good evening. What a beautiful
night. You look lonely.'

JIM: When's the punchline?

TOM: Do you mind? We're trying to do a play.

JIM: Sorry.

TOM: Thanks. Go on.

CORAL: 'You look lonely. Let's take a walk together.'

TOM: 'Let me buy you a drink, What'll you have?'

CORAL: 'Gin. No ice.'

TOM: So they fell in love almost at once.

[*They embrace passionately. She disappears behind the curtain.*]

CORAL: 'See ya later.'

TOM: 'But what shall I do? I am a ghost and she a mortal
woman with a strange power over me. I shall leave this
place. I will take a tramp steamer to Tierra del Fuego.'
But as the ship was leaving the dock ...

[CORAL's *face appears, grief stricken. She waves a handkerchief
and wails.*]

'Get back, get back.'

[*A splash.*]

She has thrown herself into the water and is swimming after the ship.

[CORAL *disappears.*]

'She will surely perish.' But just then the god of the sea took pity on her and turned her into —

[*The curtain opens to reveal* CORAL *with her legs concealed by a towel in the appropriate shape.*]

... a mermaid. So she wouldn't drown.

CORAL: 'Alas, alas, I have no legs; but at least I can follow my beloved whither he will sail. But it is so cold here on the silent bottom of the deep, and so lonely. I dwell with the denizens of the ocean, the whales, the stingrays, the giant clams and the slow moving coelacanth.'

JIM: The which?

CORAL: Coelacanth. It's prehistoric. 'Forever in the darkness of the sea I follow my beloved. How I yearn for the land, the sky, the grass, but to walk causes me terrible pain in my nether regions. So far from home, swimming after my ghostly lover.'

TOM: Whenever they met dockside she tried to walk to him but cried out in great pain.

CORAL: 'Alas!'

[*She swoons.*]

TOM: Finally the god of the sea took pity on them. He gave the sailor one wish. Whatever he wanted he could have. 'What shall I do? Return to human life again? Or enter heaven and end this endless wandering torture? No. It is my love who must be saved. She must return to dry land. Better I am unhappy for all eternity than she suffer another moment.' So the sailor wished that his love walk again. The god was totally amazed but granted his wish.

[*He removes the towel.* CORAL *contemplates her legs a moment then covers them with her kaftan.*]

CORAL: 'Oh, don't send me back. I want to follow you wherever you go.'

TOM: 'You don't belong here. You must return to your own world and your own people. You must no longer dwell with the whales, the stingrays, the giant clams and the slow

moving coelacanth. It's not good for you. Go back to the
land, the grass, the sand.'

CORAL: 'I cannot walk. I am afraid.'

TOM: 'I will show you how.'

> [*He lifts her and holds her as she takes a step forward, then
> another, then another.*]

CORAL: 'I'm walking.

> [*Mendelssohn's Nocturne is heard.*]

I'm walking, I'm walking.' [*In her own voice*] I'm walking,
I'm walking, I'm walking.

> [*As she disappears offstage she turns and waves to* TOM, *who
> waves back. They all watch her go. He picks up the towel, buries
> his face in it a moment then takes a bow. The applause is led
> thunderously by* GWEN. VIC *goes and looks where* TOM *and*
> CORAL *have gone. There is a great red glow offstage.*]

VIC: They've lit a bonfire on the beach. Look! It's like when
the Armada was coming.

> [*They all stand and watch the fire for a moment, then slowly
> walk off towards it.* VIC *and* HARRY *remain and leave the stage
> in another direction.*]

ACT FIVE

SCENE ONE

As the Nocturne continues to play, ROY *comes on. He looks forlorn, alone. He looks around vacantly. In another part of the stage* MEG *carries in the suitcases.* GWEN *staggers in with more things.* MEG *takes them from her and goes out.* GWEN *turns to go but stops.* JIM *comes in with the cardboard carton. He takes out a parcel and hands it to her. She unwraps it. It is a pair of slippers. She looks at them, then at him and walks away, a bit overcome.* JIM *goes to her and they embrace.* CORAL *comes in carrying her hat upside down. She approaches* ROY *cautiously. When he sees her he is confused. She approaches him and offers him the hat. He takes it. She digs her hands into the crown of the hat and lifts out a handful of shells. She lets them run through her fingers. She lifts them out again.* ROY *leans towards them and buries his face in the shells in* CORAL*'s hands. She lets them go again and picks them up. He kisses the shells and her hands.* JIM *and* GWEN *have left the stage.* MEG *comes in and picks up the carton and takes it off. As* ROY *and* CORAL *leave* MISS LATROBE *comes on. The light becomes bright, summery, morning.*

SCENE TWO

The schoolyard.
    MISS LATROBE *looks about her at the morning. The other actors come in.* MISS LATROBE *hands out books. They read the first scene of* King Lear *down to the entrance of the king.* MISS LATROBE *stops them.*

MISS LATROBE: I thought I'd bring you all out here under the trees to read this, in my opinion, Shakespeare's greatest tragedy. Now there are many who would give *Hamlet* pride of place, but it is the struggle between man and nature, as well as between man and man, and between man and himself that make this, for me, his masterwork. And it is the power of nature, its participation in the drama that made me bring you all outside to commence work on your text for this year. Now settle down [*as they sit in a circle*]

and we'll continue reading *King Lear* by William
Shakespeare. Tom, you're our own Chips Rafferty, why
don't you go on reading? Pick it up at the King's opening
speech.

TOM: 'Meantime we shall express our darker purpose.
　　Give me the map there. Know that we have divided
　　In three our kingdom; and 'tis our fast intent
　　To shake all cares and business from our age,
　　Conferring them on younger strengths, while we
　　Unburden'd crawl toward death.'
　　[*They remain still as the lights fade, the closing bars of
　　Mendelssohn's music are heard. Beyond them, as in a dream,
　　the lights play on the blue horizon and the sea.*]

THE END

Above: Eilish Wahren (Meg), Judie Douglass (Gwen), Bill le Marquand (Harry), Yvonne Martin (Vic) and Stephen Lovatt (Tom) in the Court Theatre production, Christchurch, New Zealand, 1988. Photo by Lloyd Park. Below: Christian Hodge (Tom) in the Griffin Theatre Company production 1986. Photo by Francisco Vidinha.